G000066658

COUTURE
DOGS
OF NEW YORK

PAUL NATHAN

COUTURE DOGS OF NEW YORK

PAUL NATHAN

PELLUCEO

© 2013 Pelluceo
www.pelluceo.com

Front and back cover images: Paul Nathan
Designed by: Gabriela Bornstein
Previous page: Portia wears an evening gown by Maggie Norris Couture.

Printed in China

ISBN: 978-0-9851368-1-9

10 9 8 7 6 5 4 3 2

For Alexa, age 1, who said "Wo-Wo" every time she saw a dog during the production of this book.

Introduction

New York, NY

In most cities around the world, Valentine's Day is a big night. In Manhattan you can be sure that every socialite has a fabulously chic charity ball or dinner to attend with red carpet entrances flanked by paparazzi. Thousands of dollars will be spent in preparation: Finding the perfect outfit, primping hair and nails.

However socialites are not the only city dwellers with a full calendar at this time of year. New York's couture dogs have equally packed social schedules, not to mention to-do lists that include fittings with fashion designers and appointments at parlors and spas (dogs need manicures and pedicures to look their best too. See page 24).

Take Eli Biehl, or "Eli the celebrity Chihuahua," as he prefers to be called. Last year, just days before the 136th Annual Westminster Kennel Club Dog Show made its way to Madison Square Garden, he and his "Mom," Karen Biehl (the pair are stars on the reality TV series *Doggie Moms*), were prepping for the Pre-Westminster Fashion Show and party that was held on February 14th at the Penn Top Ballroom at the pet-friendly Hotel Pennsylvania in midtown, to benefit New York City shelter animals.

Not only did Eli look fabulous, he had a very important role to play: On this night of romance, several "puptials" (wedding ceremonies for dogs) would be officiated by him and Karen. "When Eli and I met, both of our lives changed for the better," says Karen. "Together we have a mission to bring fun, entertainment, inspiration and joy to others."

Photographer Paul Nathan had just started documenting New York's best-dressed dogs when he attended the Pre-Westminster Fashion Show. There, along with Karen and Eli, he met famous doggie couturiers Anthony Rubio of Bandit Rubio Designs (see page 19) and Roberto Negrin of Hec-lin Couture. The latter wore peacock feather-inspired face paint to match his Poodle, Hec-lin's outfit (see page 38).

For Paul, it was the beginning of an incredible journey into the New York "Doggie World." His Facebook friends list immediately expanded to include at least 10 dogs and he began to receive invitations to "pawties"—everything from themed events like the "1001 Arabian Nights Dog Wedding and Bark Bazaar" (see page 126) to pet fashion shows on the Coney Island boardwalk (see page 74). "New York is now legendary for having the most dog related events from weddings to fund raisers to competitions," says Anthony. "Last year I created eight garments for the wedding party of what has now become the world record-breaking, most expensive dog wedding in history." He is referring, of course, to the $250,000 marriage of Baby Hope Diamond, a teacup-sized Coton de Tulear, to Chilly Pasternak, a poodle. The pair were joined in holy "muttrimony" at a black-tie gala held in the Jumeirah Essex House overlooking Central Park. Wendy Diamond, Baby Hope's owner, threw the over-the-top puptials to raise money for the Humane Society of New York. Tickets went for $200 a head.

But not all the pawties are open to the public. If you're a member of the Doggie World, you will also be invited to Barkmitvahs, yappy hours, and ice cream socials in the form of meetups, most famously the Chihuahua meetups hosted by pet fashion designer Ada Nieves. "I design outfits for red carpet events, fundraisers, doggie bridal showers and weddings, dogs blessings, and Bark days," says Roberto.

While socializing with the four-legged, Paul photographed married pooches who wear matching outfits to hail yellow cabs (see page 118-119) and visited the homes of dog owners with walk-in closets filled with enough designer outfits for their respective pups to rival any New York fashionista (see pages 48 and 90). Eventually he chose fifteen of the most stylish hounds to invite to his studio along with their favorite couture outfits to pose for this book. Take a look at *Doggie Moms* star Grace Forster's Chihuahua, Portia in a gorgeous beaded evening gown by Maggie Norris Couture, a couturier who usually focuses on the two-legged (see page 2), and in a Bandit Rubio gown inspired by the tribute to fashion designer Alexander McQueen at the Metropolitan Museum of Art in New York (see page 57).

The result is a giddily glamorous romp with some of New York's most "pawsome" pups. And because some of the dogs themselves were rescued from shelters and most of the events they dress up for benefit animal charities, we can't help but applaud the fabulous Cinderella-like quality that their lives have taken on ever since they met up with their "doggie parents."

And for those who raise an eyebrow at a pooch dressed to the "k-nines," rest assured: "Being an animal lover, I take into consideration the comfort and safety of the subject I am designing for," says Anthony. "I refuse to use chemicals or glues that may prove harmful. I use fabrics that are lightweight, will not shed any harmful decorations that the dog could swallow, and will breathe and move with the animal."

From day to eveningwear to red carpet-worthy numbers and the odd costume (see the *Black Swan* on page 37, Elvis on page 16, and Marilyn Monroe on page 122), Paul has captured the city's most fashionable tail-waggers strutting their finest, mostly made-to-order stuff.

Ladies and Gentlemen, we give you *Couture Dogs of New York*.

Nadine Rubin Nathan

This page: Portia wears a dress and hat by Bandit Rubio Designs by Anthony Rubio.
Opposite: Eli wears Ada Nieves for Pets.

indognito
Canines in Costume

2012

ELI
TIMES SQUARE DOG DAY MASQUERADE
WINNER 2007

This page: Eli wears Hec-lin Couture by Roberto Negrin, hat by Luna's Brat Pack by Ninoska Viggiano.
Opposite: Karen Biehl, *Doggie Moms* reality TV star and pro bono coordinator and Eli, Upper West Side.

Karen Biehl

"Doggie Moms" reality TV star,
pro bono coordinator and mom to Eli,
the Celebrity Chihuahua

Number of outfits: More than I can count—hundreds. Eli has been given outfits by fans and also as a result of modeling, and also has custom made outfits designed by the top NYC designers.

When did you first become a dog owner?
I adopted Eli from Craigslist in July of 2005. I am his third owner.

How did you come to start dressing him up?
When I first adopted Eli, I bought him clothes instantly. I had seen *Legally Blonde* and loved the message behind the movie—to go for your dreams regardless of your appearance and the way others perceive you. I also loved the way Bruiser in the film dressed. The first time I put a shirt on Eli, he lifted his paws and put them through the armholes. It was clear to me that he was used to wearing doggie clothes. About six months after I adopted him, I entered him in a beauty pageant, and it was incredibly fun to prepare for the different sections—formal wear, casual wear and talent. When Eli aced his talent, I got chills because I knew he would win, and I also knew that this was just the start of something amazing. He did win and as a result ended up in a full spread in *New York Dog* magazine modeling dog clothes. It was so fun that I entered him in more contests, landing him on the cover of the *MilkBone* box from 2007-2008. From then, his career skyrocketed. The outfits had a lot to do with it. He has also appeared in a fall fashion issue of *Vogue* and modeled in ads for Bank of America, Bloomingdales and others. He is even listed in the IMDb.

What was Eli's very first outfit?
A turquoise and white striped T-shirt that said "Lucky" on the back in bling. I bought this for him on the day I adopted him, and he wore it to his first dog event the next day, which was a Chihuahua meetup group ice cream social hosted by the fashion designer Ada Nieves.

What is the most you've ever spent on an outfit for Eli?
For Eli, $300, but we often have combined outfits that match, which makes the cost go up. I have spent upwards of $1000 during Halloween for our matching outfits and accessories, because one costume is not enough for all the events we attend at that time of year.

Who are Eli's favorite designers?
Eli wears mostly Hec-lin Couture by Roberto Negrin, Ada Nieves for Pets by Ada Nieves, and Bandit Rubio Designs by Anthony Rubio.

Where is the best place to show off Eli in New York?
New York is rife with formal dog events that are fundraisers for animal rescues and charities, like Bideawee, North Shore, the Humane Society and many others. Eli and I are regulars at these high-end events, which usually have a red carpet. For this reason, and because I tend to match and color coordinate with his outfits, photos of Eli in his outfits have ended up in the news on TV, in newspapers and in photographs for wire services. Eli has also modeled at many of these charity events and also at professional runway shows.

What other events do you regularly attend?
Eli and I have performed five dog weddings for animal charities to date, and we participate every year in the American Cancer Society's Bark for Life dog walk, for which Eli has raised $14,000 since 2006. We also enjoy outdoor dog event festivals, yappy hours, dog swims, beach parties, birthday parties, and dog pageants and contests. If an event exists for humans, it also exists for

dogs in NYC. The same goes for doggie couture. If it has been made for a human, it has been made for a dog.

How did you first find out about the events and parties?
Through Ada Nieves' Chihuahua meetup group— she sends announcements about events.

What does being an active member of the dog community add to your life?
It adds lots of fun. The satisfaction of making people happy, or even making them see things in a different way, and opportunities to get involved in helping raise money for those animals that are suffering or need homes.

Do you see Eli as a pet or a "fur child?"
Eli is neither of these: He is my soul mate. When we met, both of our lives changed for the better. Together we have a mission to bring fun, entertainment, joy and inspiration to others. There are several who have followed our lead and become involved in the fun.

What do your friends and family think of your role in doggie fashion events?
They are amazed by all that we have been able to accomplish, by how often Eli appears in the press and on TV, by the money he has raised for charities, and by how my life has transformed as a result.

Can you share the rudest comment you've ever heard about Eli?
After Eli was all over the press wearing his pope outfit made for him by Roberto Negrin of Hec-lin Couture, I received a very angry email on Facebook that read, "You blasphemer! How dare you, woman, defile our religion." That particular outfit created a lot of buzz on the Internet.

"The first time I put a shirt on Eli he lifted his paws and put them through the armholes. It was clear to me that he was used to wearing doggie clothes."

This page and opposite: Z Zee in Pame Derr for Laceys Elite Boutique at the
1,001 Arabian Nights Dog Wedding and Bark Bazaar event in midtown Manhattan.

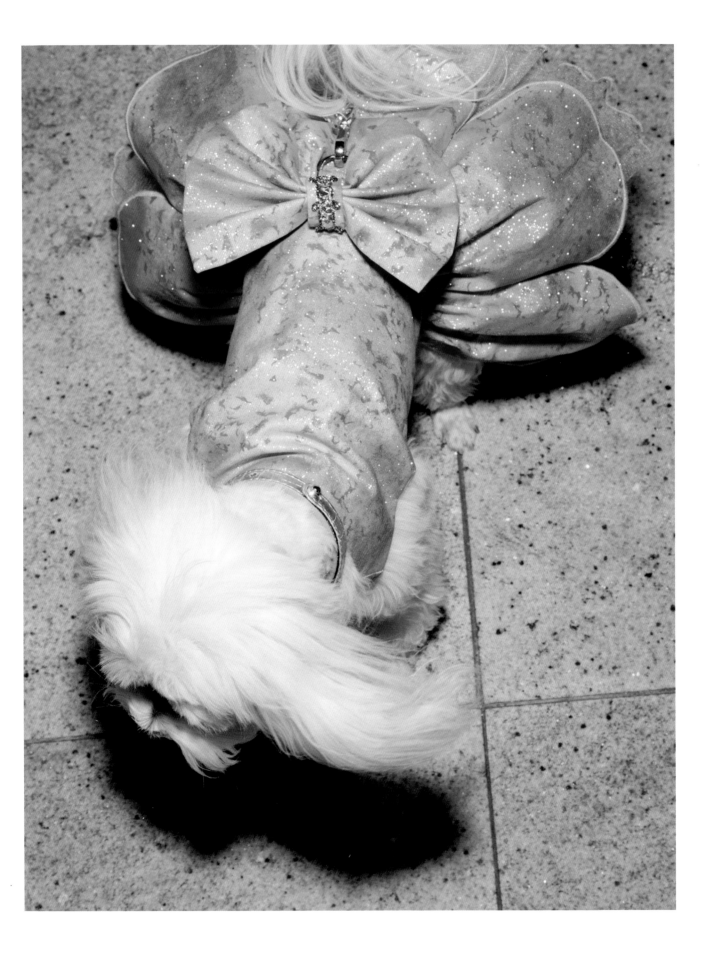

This page: Athena wears Hec-lin Couture by Roberto Negrin.
Opposite: Cory Van Den Bossche, breath and meditation teacher and Alexi, Pomerainian, Upper East Side.

This page: Chihuahuas Bogie and Kimba wear Bandit Rubio Designs by Anthony Rubio.
Opposite: Anthony Rubio, pet couturier with Kimba and Bogie, the Flatiron District.

This page and opposite: Portia wears an evening gown and hat by Bandit Rubio Designs by Anthony Rubio.

This page: Sofia Pietra, Maltese, wears Lady B. Couture and Gabriella Rosetta, Yorkie, wears Haute Puppy.
Opposite: Kim Valentini, entrepreneur with Sofia Pietra and Gabriella Rosetta, Midtown East.

This page: Z Zee wears Tammy Peace for Pampered Pets Boutique.
Opposite: Ilene Zeins and Z Zee at the Mardi Paws event in midtown Manhattan.

This page: Tasha, Morkie, and Cuba, Havanese, wear Tammy Peace for Pampered Pets Boutique.
Opposite: Bob Shaughnessy, owner of PawVogue.com and Cuba with Susan Godwin, actor, and Tasha, Chelsea.

Bob Shaughnessy

Owner of retail web site PawVogue.com and dad to Cuba, Havanese.

Number of outfits: A hundred plus, but we recently gave away about a third of Cuba's clothes.

When did you first become a dog owner?
I have always had dogs in my life but as an adult Cuba is my second dog.

How did you come to start dressing Cuba in designer clothing?
As a puppy Cuba had a few winter coats and sweaters, but at about age 1 a friend gave him a gorgeous Ralph Lauren sweater. That sweater looked so handsome on him, that it really started the trend.

What is the most you've ever spent on an outfit for Cuba?
Cuba has quite a few outfits in the $600 range.

Who are Cuba's favorite designers?
I plead the Fifth! I own PawVogue.com which showcases twenty-five pet fashion designers, so I am not selecting favorites.

Where's the best place to show off a well-dressed dog in New York?
There are many dog charity functions throughout the year where you will find most dogs dressed up. However, if you are looking for attention from outside of the dog community, any major tourist attraction in Manhattan will do.

How do you stay on top of the events?
Cuba was NYC Top Dog in 2010, so he is very well known locally. Nationally he is well known too as he also won the America's Top Dog Award and the Top Ten Dogs on Facebook award. He also does modelling to raise money for dog shelters. He gets invited to all the events.

What does being an active member of the dog community add to your life?
I am very involved in two dog communities: One is a web site I started almost five years ago, DP-Family (Dogs+People+Family)—a private dog social site which is free and has over 300 members from around the world. This group has an annual four-day weekend in a different city each year. Now I also own PawVogue, a pet fashion portal for designers and dogs who love to wear designer clothes. Many of the members overlap into both groups and a few of them have become my very best friends.

Do you see Cuba as a pet or a "fur child?"
I do not like the term "fur children." Dogs are not children with fur. Havanese have hair, not fur, anyway so is Cuba a "hair child?" I think of him just as a member of the family.

What do people think of your role in doggie fashion events?
Most would say I am over the top, as is the dog world. Until they attend an event and realize it is not much different than any other type of organization (except we have our dogs with us). Attending a fashion event is also a way to raise money for a dog shelter, and almost everyone supports raising money for dog shelters.

Have you ever encountered rudeness when Cuba is all dressed up?
I have never had a rude comment. It is always the opposite—"How adorable!"

What is the biggest compliment?
The first time we took Cuba and his then-girl-friend (now wife), Tasha, to see the Christmas tree at Rockefeller Center, they had on cute little Christmas outfits. We had them sit and stay for some photos. The tourists lined up to take photos of them. They were being photographed more than the tree!

Susan Godwin

*Actor and mom to Tasha Bella, Morkie
(Maltese/Yorkie)*

Number of outfits: Hundreds.

When did you first become a dog owner?
January 2007. Tasha is my first.

How did you come to start dressing Tasha?
I took Tasha to her first meetup at the suggestion of her Puppy School teacher to start socializing her. Tasha was the only naked dog in the room. It was so embarrassing! That's when I realized that New York dogs dress to impress. I immediately went online and googled "dog clothes."

What was her very first outfit?
A pink coat—to get her used to wearing something before I started her in dresses. She was so distracted on her walk, with all the New York city smells and greeting other dogs, that she wasn't bothered by wearing a coat. Soon she started associating wearing clothes with going out and having fun. So now her tail wags when I even pick up one of her dresses.

What is the most you've spent on an outfit?
$375.

Who are Tasha's favorite designers?
Tammy Peace for Pampered Pets Boutique, Lady B Couture, Toni Mari, Lil Yorkie Fru Fru by Kelly Owens, Ada Nieves for Pets, and Hec-lin Couture by Roberto Negrin.

Where's the best place to show Tasha off?
Fifth Avenue, of course! And the Pre-Westminster Fashion Show event—that's the party of the year.

What does being an active member of the dog community add to your life?
Having Tasha has changed my life. She gives me unconditional love and in return I give her the best of everything. She is my little girl and it brings me much joy to dress her everyday and see the smiles that she brings to people on the streets of New York and at events. Tasha now works as a model/dog actress. She has been on *Law & Order*, *Old Dogs*, and *Tower Heist*, among others. Yes, I've put my child in the family business! The fact that she doesn't mind dressing up has gotten her more work. I am a very proud mom. We truly enjoy our life together.

What do your friends and family think of your role in doggie fashion events?
My friends and family thought it odd at first but now my parents even carry Tasha's business card around and brag about their "granddaughter Tasha Bella" to their friends. My brother, who prefers cats, has even started buying Tasha clothes for her birthday and Christmas. We've come a long way!

Can you share the rudest comment you've ever heard about Tasha?
It was a warm Spring day but by no means 100 degrees or anything (I wouldn't put Tasha in any danger or make her suffer in the heat, just for fashion's sake). A woman walking behind us said, loudly enough for me to hear her, "Oh my God, the poor dog is dying of heat and then she makes *it* wear that hideous outfit on top of it!" Then a "friend" put on Facebook, for all the world to see, "Stop dressing your dog and get a real child." That person has been unfriended.

Do you see Tasha as a pet or a "fur child"?
Tasha is my only child.

This page: Tasha wears Tammy Peace for Pampered Pets Boutique. Hat by Roni Goldberg.
Opposite: Laura Lobdell, jewelry designer and Xiao Loong, Japanese Chin, Greenwich Village.

This page: Cuba wears Tammy Peace for Pampered Pets Boutique.
Opposite: Anthony Rubio with Bogie and Kimba in Bandit Rubio Designs.

Anthony Rubio

Award winning pet couturier,
Bandit Rubio Designs

Dogs: Kimba Rubio (blonde) and Bogie Rubio (brunette), Chihuahua twins.

How many outfits do Kimba and Bogie each own: 52 each and growing.

When did you first become interested in fashion design?

As a child I was enamored with classic movies. I took an interest in the way clothing played a role in these films and I guess that's when I caught the bug. My mom was a very fashionable lady. Growing up in the most fashion forward times in history I loved to watch her keep up with all the trends from bell bottoms and mini skirts to platform shoes and big hair. She had impeccable taste. Every occasion was like theater—watching all of the selections and preparations waiting in total anticipation for the big "reveal." And she never disappointed. Her love of fashion rubbed off on me.

When did you first begin designing clothing for dogs?

I started designing for dogs after discovering that a Chihuahua I had rescued had a penchant for clothes. I named him Bandit and he inspired my first work—an Elvis outfit complete with cape and sunglasses, which he wore proudly parading like a true little show off. In that outfit Bandit became an icon in the canine community and eventually worldwide. He also took on Michael Jackson and Lady Gaga just to name a few of his personas. He even went on television as the infamous Donald Trump sporting a combover wig. After he passed away I got my two boys, Kimba Rubio and Bogie Rubio. They have picked up where Bandit left off, keeping his legacy alive. These two are now "celebri-pups" having appeared in theater and on the famous New York Fashion Week runway as well as at many events and fundraisers to help raise awareness for those pups less fortunate.

Did you have to study to learn how to design for dogs?

I attended New York's Fashion Institute of Technology (FIT) majoring in women's wear design. I could not afford, at that time, to pursue fashion design further by flying to Europe for apprenticeship and decided on another career. It was Bandit who inspired me to design again and, with careful studying of the anatomy of the four-legged, I converted my design knowledge into designing for dogs. My designs can also be worn by cats.

What are some of the challenges of designing for the four-legged?

Being an animal lover, I take into consideration the comfort and safety of the subject I am designing for. I refuse to use chemicals or glues that may prove harmful. I use fabrics that are lightweight, will not shed any harmful decorations that the dog could swallow, and will breathe and move with the animal. Unlike clothes for people, these designs cover only the back part of the dog so that they are able to handle their biological needs without interruption or danger of ruining the garment. Most of the noticeable decorations and folds, pleats or tucks have to be done on the visual side, that being the back. Decorations can also be applied and emphasized on the collars and in the front, dangling from the neck area. .

How would you describe your label?

My label is couture. I make everything myself—from the beginning sketches to the actual draping then on to the construction which is ultimately hand embellished. It takes hours of labor.

Who are your style icons?

After visiting the Alexander McQueen exhibit at the Metropolitan Museum of Art I was inspired to create several outfits that celebrate his works and his aesthetic as well as those of world-renowned milliner Phillip Treacy. Mr. Treacy, who created the fascinators for the guests at the recent Royal wedding in England, has influenced my hats immensely. Other inspirations are John Galliano for the House of Dior and Thierry Mugler.

How else do you find inspiration?

I find inspiration in just about everything. I am influenced by classic architecture and fine art, especially because of my extensive travels through Europe.

Do you have a muse?

Bandit was my original muse. Now Bogie and Kimba are the muses. I also have lots of muses in the dogs of my clients and friends. Sometimes I create and call the owners up to tell them what their dogs have inspired and they are thrilled.

What are some of the events that you have created outfits for?

New York is legendary for having the most dog related events from weddings and fund raisers to competitions. Just recently I created eight garments for the wedding party of what has now become the world record-breaking, most expensive dog wedding in history ($250,000).

What's out when it comes to dressing dogs?

If the dog cannot walk correctly or if the garment is cumbersome and awkward, falling to the side or causing the dog to want to rip it off, that would be classified as "out" in my opinion. I also do not see why anyone would want to glue anything on an animal for fashion's sake, be it a bow, jewels, or eyelashes.

What is the most you've ever billed for one of your outfits?

Many of my clients would rather I kept that confidential. I can say that I have gone into the upper hundreds. The sky is the limit when it comes to couture. I have done garments in the best silks and used actual crystals.

Do you ever make an amazing outfit for another dog and wish you'd kept it for Bogie or Kimba?

I have created pieces that have blown me away. I put my heart and my soul into every garment I create and I call them "my babies." To part with them, even at the highest price, still hurts a little so I say that my clients have adopted my children. Still, I take great pride when I see my creations paraded and when they get the acknowledgement and appreciation they each deserve.

Have you ever received criticism from the public for what you do?

I think it's a lack of education or appreciation when people stop and say things like, "Dogs are not supposed to wear clothes." I have also heard things like, "That's ridiculous" or, "Why would a dog wear sunglasses?" I say, different strokes for different folks. In this country we are allowed the freedom of expression and if I want my pets or my clients to be a form of my expression, then so be it. By the way, the sunglasses protect their eyes from harmful UV rays just like for people.

What is the greatest compliment?

When people tell me that they wish that someone would create something this special for them. I recently delivered a garment to a client at an event. She told me to create what I wanted for her dog. When she opened the box she just gushed. She took that garment out and showed it to everyone she encountered bragging about its magnificence. It wasn't even on the dog!

This page: Boo, Toy Poodle, wears a *Black Swan*-inspired dress and mask by Hec-lin Couture by Roberto Negrin.
Opposite: Audrey Reagin, pet therapist and real estate agent, and Boo.

This page: Eli wears Hec-lin Couture by Roberto Negrin.
Opposite: Roberto Negrin and Hec-lin at the Pre-Westminster Fashion Show at Hotel Pennsylvania, midtown Manhattan.

Previous pages: At the Pre-Westminster Fashion Show at Hotel Pennsylvania, midtown Manhattan.
This page and opposite: Gucci wears couture gowns by Olga Zabelinska.

This page: Portia wears a dress by Hec-lin Couture by Roberto Negrin. Hat by Roni Goldberg.
Opposite: Starr Haymes Kempin, interior designer and Sugar, Malti-Poo, Upper East Side.

This page: Portia wears a dress and head piece by Hec-lin Couture by Roberto Negrin.
Opposite: Eli wears Ada Nieves for Pets.

This page: Eli wears Hec-lin Couture by Roberto Negrin.
Opposite: Ilene Zeins, real estate broker and Z Zee, Malti-Poo, Bergen Beach, Brooklyn.

Ilene Zeins
Real estate broker and doggie mom
to Z Zee, Malti-Poo

Number of outfits: Approximately 75.

When did you first become a dog owner?
In August 2008, when I got Z Zee.

How did you come to start dressing Z Zee?
As soon as I got Z Zee, I bought some things for her—a little dress and T-shirts from Target. In 2011 when I took Z Zee to the Pre-Westminster Fashion Show, I was amazed by the styles I saw around me. I discovered doggie designers and I wanted Z Zee to be a Wannabe Super Model. That was the beginning for me. I created a Facebook page for Z Zee, started friending lots of people and pups, and I started watching what the most fashionable dogs were wearing. And, well, we started to go shopping…

What was her very first designer outfit?
A pink and green polka dot dress from designer Tammy Peace for Pampered Pets Boutique.

What is the most you've ever spent on an outfit for Z Zee?
I spent $250 on a harness in black Italian leather with a faux fur trim.

Favorite designers?
Anthony Rubio of Bandit Rubio Designs, Tammy Peace for Pampered Pets Boutique, Ada Nieves of Ada Nieves Designs for Pets, Linda Higgins, Sandra Barnes of Chicka-Bow-Wow.

How do you stay on top of the trends?
We stay on top of the trends via Facebook. I am friends with many designers and some will post a photo on Z Zee's page if something new comes out. Of course from time-to-time I contact a designer to design a needed outfit, whether it be for an event or something special. For instance, I just had a beautiful outfit made from the skirt of a suit that was originally owned by my mom—the designer reproduced the look of it and it is very precious to me.

What does being an active memeber of the dog community add to your life?
I have made many, many new friends both in New York, the country and overseas. I try to spend Saturdays with Z Zee since I work all week and I rather enjoy the planning of the Saturday, thinking about Z Zee's outfit, what the other "girls" are wearing and where we will go to have lunch etc. It has extended beyond just dressing her up for a special event.

Do you see dogs as pets or "fur children?"
I hate the expression "fur children." Z Zee is a member of the family. I'll leave it at that!

What do friends and family think of your role in doggie fashion events?
They think I spend entirely too much time dressing Z Zee up. "Let her be a dog," they say. While everybody loves Z Zee's photos, remarks have been made that I have totally lost it because all I post on Facebook is about Z Zee.

Can you recall the best compliment Z Zee has ever been paid?
The best compliment was when we won first prize in the Celebrity Catwalk Mardi-Paws event for dressing alike. That was totally unexpected.

"I had a beautiful outfit made for Z Zee from the skirt of a suit that was originally owned by my mom—the designer reproduced the look of it and it is very precious to me."

This page: Portia wears gown and flower head piece by Deni Alexander Designs.
Opposite: Portia wears gown and top hat by Deni Alexander Designs.

This page: Gucci wears a couture gown by Olga Zabelinskaya.
Opposite: Caroline Loevner, brand manager and Beau, Husky, Upper East Side.

This page: Tasha and Cuba wear Tammy Peace for Pampered Pets Boutique.
Opposite: Grace Forster with Rosie and Portia at the Mardi Paws event in Midtown, Manhattan.
Rosie and Portia wear Alexander McQueen-inspired gowns and hats by Bandit Rubio Designs by Anthony Rubio.

This page: Athena wears Hec-lin Couture by Roberto Negrin.
Opposite: Roberto Negrin, pet couturier with DJ and Athena, Chihuahuas, Bronx.

Roberto Negrin

Fashion designer, Hec-lin Couture for Dogs

Dogs: Hec-lin (toy Poodle), DJ (Chihuahua), Abby (Yorkie mix), Athena (Chihuahua)

How many outfits each: Not as much as I wish.

When did you first become interested in fashion design?
I come from a little town called San Francisco de Macoris in the Dominican Republic. I grew up seeing my mom sewing, painting, baking, always fixing and re-decorating things. I guess fashion was already in my blood.

When did you first begin designing clothing for dogs?
Everything began with my desire to enter a fun beauty pageant for dogs. I needed to bring three changes of clothing for my poodle, Hec-lin, and I wanted them to be the most fabulous. With my mother helping me to sew (even though she doesn't like dogs), Hec-lin as model to help us figure out the pattern, and my taste for fashion we made three fabulous outfits that helped us win best active wear and first runner up for the crown. We might not have won the pageant but we got so much more than that. That's when I started to use the sewing machine to make all of my ideas come to life.

Did you have to study to learn to design for the four-legged?
I never took sewing or designing classes. My mom taught me how to use the sewing machine and the rest has been a fun accident.

What are some of the challenges of designing for dogs?
When it comes to pets many challenges are involved, from choosing the appropriate fabrics that will not mess up their coats to choosing the right colors and making sure the garments fit well and are comfortable.

How would you describe your label?
The architectural style of Alexander McQueen and the Latin flavor of Oscar de la Renta.

Do you have a muse?
My babies DJ, Hec-lin, Abby and Athena are my muses. They are my reason to wake up everyday.

What are some of the events that clients commission outfits for?
From red carpet events, fundraisers, doggie showers, bridal showers and weddings to dogs blessings, Bark days and any other themed events.

What's in when it comes to dressing dogs?
Fashion changes every season for humans as well as for dogs. My job is just to make fashion fun for my clients and their dogs.

What is the most you've ever billed a client for an outfit?
My most expensive creation so far cost $500.

Do you ever make amazing outfits for other dogs and wish you'd kept them?
Every single design is a new adventure for me. When I get inspired by my clients' dogs I put myself so into the creation. Its like I'm making the outfit for one of my own babies.

What is the funniest comment you've ever heard about what you do?
That I dress up my dogs because I was not able to dress up Barbie dolls when I was kid.

How about the rudest?
That what I'm doing isn't right because pets cannot be treated like humans.

"My babies DJ, Hec-lin, Abby and Athena are my muses. They are my reason to wake up everyday."

This page: Hec-lin wears Hec-lin Couture by Roberto Negrin.
Opposite: Shakyra LaShae, model and Sasha Leona, Imperial Shitzu, Dumbo, Brooklyn.

This page: Z Zee wears Tammy Peace for Pampered Pets Boutique.
Opposite: At the 1,001 Arabian Nights Dog Wedding and Bark Bazaar event, midtown Manhattan.

This page: Eli wears Wiggles. Opposite: Jesse Fischler, project manager and tour manager and Angelo, Chihuahua, East Village.

This page: Athena wears Hec-lin Couture by Roberto Negrin. Opposite: Dave Sutton, writer and Victoria Masters, art director and photographer with Bean, Miniature Pinscher, Williamsburg, Brooklyn.

This page: Meeka wears jacket by Monkey Daze, scarf by OoMaLoo, and denim skirt and shirt by Dog In The Closet.
Opposite: Jocelyn Brandeis, dog community writer and Madison, Toy Poodle, Upper East Side.

This page: Z Zee wears Tammy Peace for Pampered Pets Boutique.
Opposite: Erica Stein, design writer and web designer and Sir Chesterfield Sundae Latte Coco Puff Montgomery,
Miss Georgia Peach Ball Fizzy Moon, and Mr Cosmo Kramer, Chihuahuas, Greenwich Village.

This page: Tasha wears Hec-lin Couture by Roberto Negrin.
Opposite: At the Pet Fashion Show, Coney Island, Brooklyn.

This page: Kimba and Bogie wear Bandit Rubio Designs by Anthony Rubio.
Opposite: Amy Yu, marketing manager and Soba, Maltese/Poodle, East Harlem.

This page: Tasha and Cuba wear Tammy Peace for Pampered Pets Boutique.
Opposite: Cuba wears Tammy Peace for Pampered Pets Boutique.

This page: Eli wears a hat by Barking Baby. Opposite: Marcia Baker and Pistachio, Miniature Pinscher mix, East Harlem.

This page: Z Zee wears Jazzies InsPAWrations.
Opposite: Luis Veronese, magazine editor with Gigi and Rocco, Dachshunds, Long Island City.

This page: Tasha wears Chica-BowWow by Sandra Barnes.
Opposite: Brett Stephan, restaurant manager and Napoleon, Yorkie, Upper West Side.

This page: BB wears Michelle Miller.
Opposite: BB wears outfit and cap by FuFu Fashions.

This page: Tommy T wears Felicia Miracolo.
Opposite: At the Pre-Westminster Fashion Show at Hotel Pennsylvania, midtown Manhattan.

This page: BB wears Michelle Miller.
Opposite: Bobbi Mitchell, executive secretary and Betty Boop aka BB, Maltese, Bronx.

Bobbi Mitchell

Executive secretary and mom to Betty Boop (aka BB), Maltese

Number of outfits: 75 to 125 (I have never actually counted).

When did you first become a dog owner?
BB is my third baby. I had a German shepherd when I was 20 and a pit bull when I was 30.

How did you come to start dressing BB?
I wanted to take her to the Pre-Westminster Fashion Show and you can't take your baby there naked. That was the beginning of the end for me!

What was BB's very first outfit?
A black and white Chanel-inspired dress that she wore to the Pre-Westminster Fashion Show. BB got her picture taken and put on the web site in it. It was a proud moment for both of us. Her very first couture outfit was a one-of-a-kind Hec-lin Couture pink and gold gown made especially for her. She won an Honorable Mention in the Barking Beauty Pageant when she wore it.

What is the most you've ever spent on an outfit for BB?
Wait, is my husband going to see this? I'm taking the Fifth!

Favorite designers?
Ada Nieves for Pets, Hec-lin Couture by Roberto Negrin, FuFuFashions, Bandit Rubio Designs by Anthony Rubio…I can go on and on.

Where's the best place to show off a well-dressed dog in New York?
Anywhere where there are people and cameras.

What does being a part of this community add to your life?
BB has a great social life and since I am her driver, I do too. I have made the best and greatest friends because of BB.

Do you see dogs as pets or "fur children?"
BB is my fur daughter.

What do your friends and family think of your role in doggie fashion events?
My friends don't know what to think, although they are amazed at BB's extensive wardrobe and her lifestyle. My parents and sister support BB in all that she does, attending her parties and shows. She is their fur grandchild and niece and they know that I would be very upset if they did not treat her as such.

Can you share the funniest comment you've ever heard about BB?
Once, when I had BB in her stroller and was waiting to go up the steps at the train station, a police officer said, "Miss, I will carry [the stroller] for you," not realizing it was BB in there. I told him I could manage, but he insisted. His partner saw the PetGear label on the stroller but didn't say anything. When the policeman got to the top of the steps he looked inside the stroller and said, "Why aren't you a little…What the hell? It's a dog!" BB just stared him right in the face. His partner and I both had tears in our eyes we were laughing so hard.

"My parents and sister support BB in all that she does, attending her parties and shows. She is their fur grandchild and niece and they know that I would be very upset if they did not treat her as such."

This page: Portia wears gown and veil by Deni Alexander Designs. Opposite: Boo wears Hec-lin Couture by Roberto Negrin.

This page: Eli wears outfit and hat by Hec-lin Couture by Roberto Negrin. Opposite:Eli wears Wiggles.

This page: Tommy T wears Felicia Miracolo.
Opposite: Kayla Soyer-Stein, writer and Frances, Chihuahua.

This page: BB wears dress and hat by Ada Nieves for Pets.
Opposite: At the Pre-Westminster Fashion Show at Hotel Pennsylvania, midtown Manhattan.

Previous pages: Roberto Negrin with Athena, Chihuahua, Abby, Yorkie mix, Hec-lin, toy Poodle, and DJ, Chihuahua.
This page: At the 1,001 Arabian Nights Dog Wedding and Bark Bazaar event, midtown Manhattan.
Opposite: Tommy T wears Hec-lin Couture by Roberto Negrin, headpiece by Felicia Miracolo.

This page: Portia wears Bandit Rubio Designs by Anthony Rubio.
Opposite: Eli wears Hec-lin Couture by Roberto Negrin.

This page: Boo wears Hec-lin Couture by Roberto Negrin. Opposite: Kate Finnegan-Prans, antique furniture restorer and artist and Frida, Chihuahua mix, Clinton Hill, Brooklyn.

This page: Tommy T wears Bandit Rubio Designs by Anthony Rubio.
Opposite: Theodore Wallach, film/creative and Ella, mix, Williamsburg, Brooklyn.

This page: Abby wears Hec-lin Couture by Roberto Negrin. Opposite: A coordinated pair in McCarren Park, Williamsburg, Brooklyn.

This page: Stella Panzarino, executive assistant and Chico, Chihuahua. Opposite: Stella and Chico, Bergen Beach, Brooklyn.

Stella Panzarino

Executive assistant, animal advocate, adoption volunteer and mom to Chico, Chihuahua (Long Coat)

Number of outfits: More than a hundred.

When did you become a dog owner?
I had dogs while growing up, but Chico is my first dog of my own. I rescued him from the back of a pet store in February 2002. (Owner? Truth be told, he owns me!)

How did you start dressing Chico?
He was my baby and he was so tiny. It was winter and I wanted to keep him warm. My sister bought him his first little sweatshirt. He looked adorable and I was immediately hooked on doggie clothes. Now he has outfits for every occasion, and I love matching our outfits—mommy and me! When I joined the NYC Chihuahua meet-up group I was exposed to a whole new world of like-minded doggie owners. Everyone dressed their doggies too, and many wore custom designer attire. Chico's wardrobe consists of casual mainstream clothes and upscale, one-of-a-kind designs, custom made by many of the top pet fashion designers.

What was his first designer outfit?
A tuxedo.

Favorite designers?
Tammy Peace for Pampered Pets Boutique, Ada Nieves for Pets, Jazzie's Inspawrations, Roni Goldberg, Roberto Negrin of Hec-lin Couture, Anthony Rubio of Bandit Rubio Designs. One of my friends, Jennifer-Jo, created the Arf Scarf—matching winter knitwear for dogs and people. It's one of our favorite matching sets.

Where's the best place to show off a well-dressed dog in New York?
The Pre-Westminster event is the highlight fashion event of the year. All the dogs are dressed to the "k-nine's," by the top designers and there's a runway show featuring designs by top designers. Halloween is also a great time to show off your dog in their best costume, many of which are created and custom designed by these top pet designers, too. But Chico is dressed whenever we go out, whether it be to meet-ups, events, fundraisers, nursing homes or a walk down the block.

What other events do you attend?
There's Bark in the Park, doggie lunch dates, birthday parties and weddings. There is always something to do in the NYC pet community.

What does being an active member of this community add to your life?
I have made many friends, not just in NYC but all over the world. It's great knowing other people who love their pets the way I love my Chico. To us it's just the norm. Maybe to some outside this circle, we're a little crazy, but our dogs are so loved and cared for; many of us are animal advocates, and we all do our best to promote that pets are truly a part of our families. We all accept each other's craziness and, in fact, we wouldn't have it any other way! Having Chico involved in the pet community has allowed me to advocate publicly for homeless animals and the need for spaying and neutering, and shelter reform. It also has given me the opportunity to simply make others smile by seeing Chico dressed in one of his outfits, and that means a lot to me.

What do your friends and family think of your role in doggie fashion events?
My friends who don't have dogs or pets of their own think I'm a little over the top, but I think they get a kick out of it. Some of my family members don't really get it. They have dogs too, but aren't part of the pet scene. I do think if they participated, they'd have a blast. But it doesn't

bother me if people think I am crazy. Maybe I am, but as long as Chico is enjoying the ride (literally since he has a stroller!). My late parents enjoyed hearing about the events and loved seeing their grand-dog Chico in his outfits, and enjoyed the attention he would get when he visited the nursing home. And they got such a thrill seeing him on TV and in the newspapers.

Can you share the rudest comment you've ever heard about Chico?
Sometimes when I have Chico in the stroller people are surprised and laugh, not expecting to see a dog in there.

What is the best compliment?
It always makes my day when people tell me that we look alike!

Do you see dogs as pets or "fur children?"
Chico is my furry son and my best friend!

"Chico is always dressed when we go out, whether it be to meet-ups, events, fundraisers, nursing homes or a walk down the block."

Previous pages: Tasha and Cuba wear Sandra Barnes of Chicka-Bow-Wow. This page: Eli wears Wiggles.
Opposite: Petey, Yorkshire Terrier, Dumbo, Brooklyn. Petey wears a suit by Petey's Closet,

This page and opposite: The incredibly versatile Tommy T wears Felicia Miracolo.

This page: Bogie and Kimba wear Bandit Rubio Designs by Anthony Rubio.
Opposite: Anthony Rubio with Kimba and Bogie at the Mardi Paws event, midtown Manhattan.

This page: Z Zee wears a dress by Tonimari. Hat by Roni Goldberg.
Opposite: Darsey Templeton Mitchell and Millie La Rue, Yorkshire Terrier, at the
1,001 Arabian Nights Dog Wedding and Bark Bazaar event, midtown Manhattan.

This page: Meeka wears outfit and hat by Lela Burton Designs for Whimsey Collection.
Opposite: Grace Forster, retired UN staff member and *Doggie Moms* reality TV star with Rosie and Portia, Yorkshire Terriers, Gramercy. Rosie and Portia wear dresses by Deni Alexander Designs. Dogs hats by Roni Goldberg.

Grace Forster

Former UN staff member, reality TV star on "Doggie Moms" and mom to Portia and Rosie, Yorkshire Terriers

Number of outfits: Hundreds for every occasion from off-the-rack numbers to custom haute couture gowns…too many to count!

When did you first become a dog owner?
In 1992 I acquired my first Yorkshire Terrier whom I named Chumley after the famous Yorkshire family "Cholmondeley."

How did you come to start dressing Portia in clothing?
Almost immediately after acquiring Chumley, I began noticing cute clothing in the dog stores. I started buying him sweaters, coats, sports T-shirts, and a leather biker jacket. Soon he had an outfit for every occasion. By the time I acquired Portia in 2005, dog couture designers had come onto the scene. I started purchasing custom-made dresses for my first female Yorkie. These days, along with Portia, I have a second Yorkie named Rosie who is equally well dressed.

What's the most you've ever spent on an outfit for Portia?
About $500 on a very special gown for a black-tie event.

Favorite designers?
Anthony Rubio of Bandit Rubio Designs, Hec-lin Couture for Dogs by Roberto Negrin, Ada Nieves of Ada Nieves for Pets, Deni Alexander Designs by Deni Alexander.

Where's the best place to show off a well-dressed dog in New York?
At an upscale, formal black-tie or red carpet benefit event with a step and repeat where there is sure to be press taking lots of photos that are likely to appear on a number of wire services like Wenn, Patrick McMullen, Getty/Wire Images, etc, in addition to Facebook.

What events do you regularly attend?
Charity benefits for animal welfare and adoption, as participants or volunteers. Portia, Rosie and I volunteer at the fun outdoor events to benefit the New Rochelle Humane Society, such as the Annual Dog Wash and Annual Hounds on the Sound. We participate in the yearly Bark for Life walk for the American Cancer Society. We act as judges for costume contests such as the 11th Hour Rescue's yearly outdoor events. We participate in various charity fashion shows throughout the year too. There are various Halloween costume parties, both outdoor and indoor, the Easter parade, meet-up groups and birthday parties throughout the year. We also attend dog-friendly events such as polo matches and art gallery openings.

How do you keep up with what is happening in the doggie world?
We are well known in the dog social scene of NYC, especially because of *Doggie Moms*. Many events are annual and I receive an invite from the host of the event or the PR firm covering the event, or a photographer assigned to the event.

Do you think of Portia and Rosie as pets or "fur children?"
My dogs are my family, not merely pets. I call them my Yorkie girls. I have a very close bond with them both, but I must admit that I see Portia whom I acquired at 6 months as my soul mate. We have been constant companions for nearly seven years.

What does being a part of this community of dressed up dogs and their owners add to your life?
It's a major part of my social life. The events are generally charity benefits, so I am not only en-

joying seeing my Yorkie girls looking glamorous and beautiful but am also contributing to animal welfare—a win-win situation. I like how it gives others pleasure to see my lovely Yorkie girls prance around in their outfits too. Through these events, we also meet photographers who ask for photo sessions, which is how many modeling jobs for my Yorkie girls are acquired. For example, Portia was asked to model for a famous animal photographer we met at a black-tie charity event, which resulted in a cover photo for the magazine *Yorkshire Terrier*, which has been on the newsstands for more than two years.

What do your family and friends think of your role in doggie fashion events?
My family thinks my role in the dog world in general is totally over-the-top, eccentric and too costly. My friends are like-minded people in the dog community, so there is no disagreement.

Can you recall the best compliment Portia has ever received?
People often comment on the fact that Portia has a more extensive wardrobe or is more groomed than themselves or their children. Everyone is amazed at how comfortable both my Yorkie girls are in hats, sunglasses, long gowns, and even footwear.

"Everyone is amazed at how comfortable my Yorkie girls are in hats, sunglasses, long gowns, and even footwear."

This page and opposite: Tasha wears KO Couture by Kelly Owens.

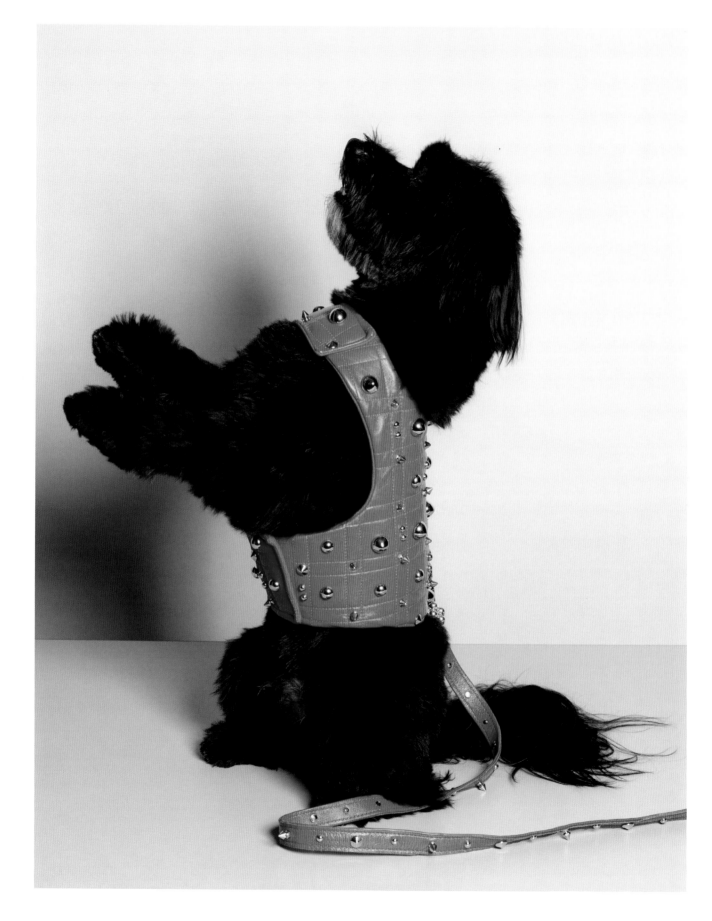

This page: Meeka wears Lena Burton Designs for Whimsey Collection. Sneakers,
Monkey Daze. Opposite: Cuba wears Rebecca Bissi of Chiencoature.

This page: Eli wears Bandit Rubio Designs by Anthony Rubio.
Opposite: Theresa Wong, floral designer and Bee Bee, Malti Poo, Chinatown.

This page: Portia wears Deni Alexander Designs, crown is home-made.
Opposite: Portia as "Medusa" in gown and head piece by Bandit Rubio Designs by Anthony Rubio.

This page: Athena wears Hec-lin Couture by Roberto Negrin.
Opposite: At the Pre-Westminster Fashion Show, Hotel Pennsylvania, midtown Manhattan.

This page: Gucci, Toy Poodle, as "Romeo". Outfit designed by Olga Zabelinskaya.
Opposite: Olga Zabelinskaya, groomer and designer and Gucci, Madison, New Jersey.

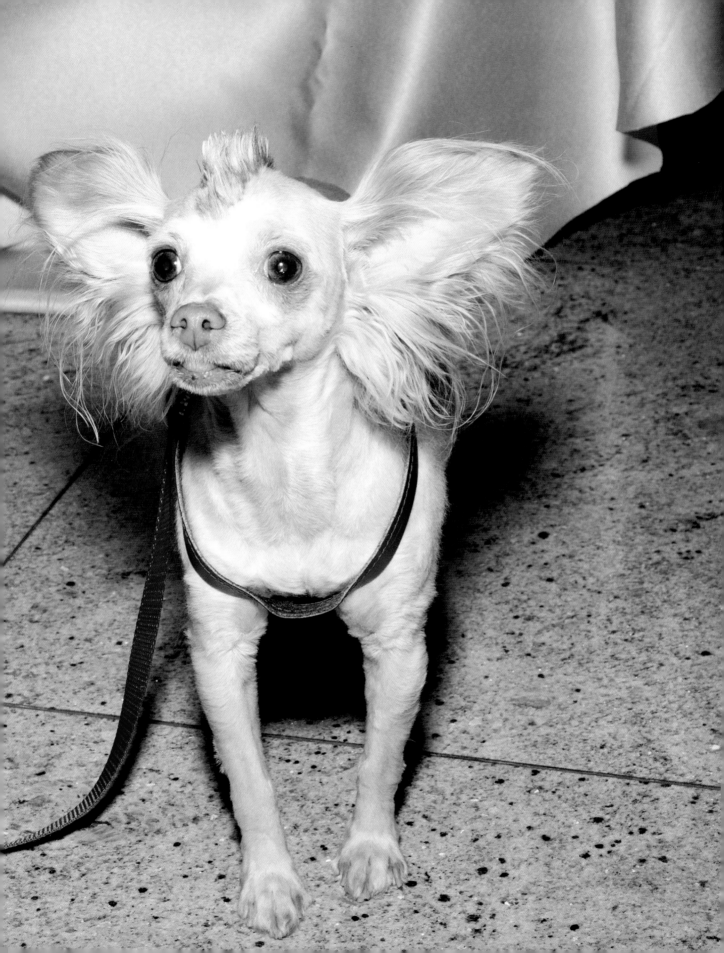

Previous pages: Tuffy at the 1,001 Arabian Nights Dog Wedding and Bark Bazaar event, midtown Manhattan. This page: Eli wears Bandit Rubio Designs by Anthony Rubio. Opposite: Christina Janssen, dogwear designer (Lady B Couture) at La Boutique Beignet and Beignet "Lady B," Maltese, Times Square.

This page: Z Zee wears Bandit Rubio Designs by Anthony Rubio.
Opposite: Eli wears Ada Nieves for Pets.

This page: Cuba wears Tammy Peace of Pampered Pets Boutique. Opposite: Ashley Speranza, *Doggie Moms* reality TV star with Max-A-Million and Misty May, Pomeranians, Bay Ridge, Brooklyn.

This page and opposite: Eli wears Hec-lin Couture by Roberto Negrin. Hat by Luna Hats.

This page: Z Zee wears Tammy Peace for Pampered Pets Boutique.
Opposite: MaryEllen Jarrell, actress and photographer with Coco and Dior, Mutts.

This page: Eli wears jacket and goggles by Wiggles. Opposite: Summer Strand, personal trainer with Daisy and Amazing Grace, Chihuahuas, Park Slope, Brooklyn.

Paul Nathan was born in Auckland, New Zealand. He has a degree in Art History and Art Theory from the University of Canterbury and is a graduate of the fulltime program at the International Center for Photography (ICP) in New York. His work has been published in books, magazines, and newspapers around the world. Prior to *Couture Dogs of New York*, he published *Generation Ink: Williamsburg, Brooklyn*.

Nadine Rubin Nathan began her career as editor-in-chief of *Elle* magazine in South Africa. After relocating to New York in 2004, she contributed to *Harper's Bazaar* and was senior editor at Assouline Publishing. Her writing has also been published in the *New York Times*. She has an MA in arts and culture journalism from Columbia University.

Paul and Nadine currently live in Williamsburg, Brooklyn with their daughter Alexa Phoebe.

A portion of the sale of this book will go to the Humane Society of New York.

Acknowledgments

The publishers wish to thank both the two-legged and the four-legged who gave up their time to pose for this book whether they appear on these pages or not. We would also like to extend a special thank you to Stella and Chico for the first introductions to the members of the New York "Doggie World."